joanne burns | amphora

New Poems

GIRAMONDO POETS

joanne burns | amphora

First published 2011
from the Writing & Society Research Group
at the University of Western Sydney
by the Giramondo Publishing Company
PO Box 752 Artarmon NSW 1570 Australia
www.giramondopublishing.com

Designed by Harry Williamson
Typeset by Andrew Davies
in 10/16.5 pt Baskerville

Printed and bound by Ligare
Distributed in Australia by the Scribo Group

National Library of Australia
Cataloguing-in-Publication data:

Burns, Joanne, 1945–

Amphora / Joanne Burns.

9781920882631 (pbk.)

A821.3

for The Shards

Other books by joanne burns:

an illustrated history of dairies
kept busy (CD)
penelope's knees (chapbook)
footnotes of a hammock
people like that
aerial photography
penelope's knees
on a clear day
blowing bubbles in the seventh lane
ventriloquy
Correspondences – with Pamela Brown
Radio City 2am – with Stefanie Bennett and Ruth K. Fordham
Adrenalin Flicknife
Alphabatics
Ratz
Snatch

Acknowledgements

Poems in this collection have appeared in: *Best Australian Poems 2006* (Black Inc), *Blast*, *Cordite Poetry Review*, *foam:e*, HEAT, *hutt*, *Ilumina*, *kept busy* (River Road), *Mascara Literary Review*, *Miel*, *Otoliths*, *Out of the Box* anthology (Puncher·& Wattman), *Poems in Conversation II*, the *Age*, The *Fine* Print.

The author would like to thank Loma Bridge for all her advice and support; and the Literature Board of the Australia Council for their financial assistance in the writing of this book via a New Work grant for 2006.

This project has been assisted by the Commonwealth Government through the Australia Council, its arts funding and advisory body.

Contents

ichoria

angles not angels

pitch

i want an angel, maybe even two,
like the ones assisting isidore, the
spanish farm servant saint, angels
who were seen to plough the fields
for him while he was deep in prayer,
i don't know exactly what they looked
like but i don't need one with that much
muscle or one from the top ranks of the angel
hierarchy and i don't want an angel with huge wings
that rustle, i need someone quiet who likes to dust and shop and
vacuum while i recline and dream up poems and skim through
dictionaries and roget's there is something about the sight
and thought of those giant angel wings in most religious art
that makes me shudder, more of a panic than rilke's terror,
like when you see a professional weightlifter walking down
the street well oiled, too much of manifested power, too
much like the sound of a punkahwallah or the sighting of
an ugg boot in a tropical land

i know an angel poem can be a cliché
but every poet's got an angel somewhere
cruising through their work even if they don't
admit it; ruffle the leaves of any old anthology
and you'll hear angels speaking through the dust

my kind of angel comes like a flash of light a silver wink in the dark a stroke of thought behind the brow down the nape of the neck so slow it's really fast. it could remind you that you're about to die if you don't shift your arse

i am waiting at the lights in darlinghurst. i have just been to the acupuncturist. i think i have a vertigo virus and am seeing an ear specialist the next day. i am in a daze but am thinking the lights are slow to change. a speeding car comes hurtling through the red lights towards me. i realise it's going to hit me and i slowly move to my right. it whooshes past me and slams into the sandstone verandah of the corner heritage house. workmen repairing the footpath rush to rescue the driver from the petrol leaking car, i look to see my imprint in the fresh black pitch on the ground. the car has missed me by five centimetres. just. i am alive. no one speaks to me and the police don't want to. have i become invisible. the soles of my feet are covered with this sticky black substance. i sway back to the acupuncturist's. in a slightly concerned trance. at least the vertigo is behaving itself. paul washes my feet clean in the february heat under the palm tree in his garden. and then i proceed back into the quotidian of the day. i *am* alive. i go and have a coffee and read vanity fair. an article on

the charisma of martha stewart. i have no delayed
reaction. i have no injury. the next week paul tells
me the street talk is of a woman seen leaping away
from the car. i did not leap. i felt too vague. in that
slow step to the right the prod of an instant angel
surely reached across to save my life

i wouldn't mind more visits from the angels
reviving slumped thoughts through my head,
electric angels, slender pins and prods of light
letting the wires of glummed imagination shine

there is an awkwardness a glibness in any
talk of angels, who wants to sound naïve, perhaps
angels are just for the more reticent parts of ourselves
particles waves antennae those parts that we can't see

and then there's the dark angel factor, the luciferous
one who descended from a star then lost its light, the bitter
angel of wormwood, absinthium, who poisoned the waters
with death; in english 'angel' can purr like a throat balm, in
spanish it sounds like 'hell'

it isn't easy to deflate the profile of a winged
angel, it seems as ancient as desire for salt, but that
flock of small winged creatures you see out of the window

may only be a hack choir of bats commuting between
the gardens and park you see them every evening
just before it gets dark

is 'psychopomp' another version of 'angel',
guiding the spirits of the living as well as
the dead, according to the oxford dictionary
of foreign words in english: this word has
the feel of a photoshopped guru touring
an international lecture in ballrooms
of five star hotels –

——

so it comes over you it never stops surprising :
after the coach tyre has blown on a mountain
side and the front light has failed again, hours later
rich as a shot of cognac waiting on a ledge in a miniature
cave a voice urges from a dark cornice down to your pillow
'enjoy' – and you did

sphere

inside the hermetic bulb
how easily it opens to
the blade, that sharp
sweet sting, mouth and
veins ring with the wash
of mercurial juice from
sheening onion flesh; it
sustained the builders of
the pyramids greek athletes
knew it lightened the balance
of the blood its shapes echoed
eternal life so the egyptians understood:
the onion's ancient history; but try to
get it in a third millennium sandwich
in a sydney café they look at you as if
you're mad as if they are afraid of it and
anyhow the customers don't want it; they'd
rather put coffee in a sandwich (toasted turkish)
or even nicorettes, why is onion getting such bad
raps; how the children of israel mourned the loss
of the onion when moses first led them into the
wilderness, just cakes of manna for dinner didn't
please them then   soft mineral and vegetable
crunch into its pristine flesh sip on the exclamation
of its juice this ichor of the gods the mind sprints
alert as an archetype: the music of the onion
as available as breath

yellow rose

they want eternal life yes salvation not damnation, yes they really want it they have offered their old watches their old strings of pearls to him to her.

at first glance at a distance the glints and gleams of their offerings instill the shrine with a theophanic glow. closer up these investments turn captive. installed behind a frosty locked glass door. icy grottophilia. could you kneel at this prie-dieu.

ropes of pearl. thin sheen of horologia. tiny habitual discs. how sad they look. no better than piles of old spectacles. walking sticks. the sadness amplified through the smells of anxiety and sincerity that circulate through the moment.

where is the divine in this tableau mort. where is the lyric of the blue tinge air. warm rush of a wilderness.

ladoo

could this be a poem
of four hands like ganesha
the hindu god who has that
many (or even fourteen)
ganesh ganapati elephant
god of good fortune wisdom
removal of obstacles sweet god of
writers, a kind of spiritual teddy
bear though never close enough for
a hug; he has his hands full with serious
things eyes black pools of a potent mind,
an elephant buddha not snuggleup bear

remover of obstacles desire & pain, one hand
holds an axe the next a whip; one hand for a blessing,
that lotus in the other realising itself: he's a handy man
no nails required, a bundle of gifts with a generous belly
that absorbs protects, a mini-pleroma a gnostic ganesh

riding his mouse, this tiny mooshikam, what does it
mean: smart rodent assistant sniffing cryptic gems,
a too proud egomind needing gee's stewardship –
a pantry of meaning, in the mythopoeisis nook;
from all accounts gee likes a ladoo or four, something
sweet to suck on as he listens for clues with those
capacious ears, vivekananda (before there were two)

i like ganesh best when he stands, one foot raised
above the ground, a fuller measure of his grace; my
unopened ganesh jigsaw puzzle gave me no obstacles
when it sat for two years below three brass figures of
his dancing self, the pieces slipped together quicker
than the washing up; he reclines on the table lit
by the shine of five ghee lamps; if you used his image
as a coaster or a placemat would he stop you eating or
drinking too much, would he take you to task –

what a task he completed with his missing tusk,
as scribe of vyasa's vast mahabharata, in his rush
to get started snapping a tusk off to use as a pen, he
never paused for a break – a true ur god
no seventh day of rest

left

there was no time left
for the picnic of lost socks
it was a century too late for
those glasses of water who
thought they had changed the
world the inner bedlamp glowing
like a capricious worm in the reverie
scrapbook; someone sat on the left
eye of the magus in underpants a
biscuit theology scattering in crumbs
through the grass; the park so groomed for
the matching poodle revolution &
the barricaded kiosk, a dilapidated god

raft

i don't know if this poem will turn out
to be a kind of carrot but it's going to have
a carrot in it, briefly   the way the carrot
appeared in one's childhood as a folksy
wisdom   *eat your carrots if you want*
to see in the dark

no one really explained
why urban children needed this aid as we all
believed in the power of electric city illumination
though seeing in the dark was a handy skill for
camping holidays and the fears of hoary monsters
unknown presences malefic spirits that quivered
inside adult exhortations

mystics like oscuridaddy san
juan de la cruz have exulted
in the dark whether harsh or
blessed as a passage a navigational
path towards divine embrace in
the chambers of god, so much passion
too much flesh and fever to reach
immersive hallowed light   a cool
flannel is needed

and hopkins with his fell of dark his
long nights of anguish   the urgency of
spiritual desires   afflictions exclamations
apostrophes may make good poems but
do they make good living

—

so much emotion swathed round this
christian god of love and loss, too much
expectation   a bad dose of country and western;
why not the dark as a place a state   let it be, like
a beatle

to hear the electric universe
hum on the spirit level quadrillions
of singing atoms   you can walk
in the dark and it brushes your skin in
endless affirmation alive in the sempiternal
you can lie in the mingling dark, certain and
calm without any personal grammar   it is
just as it is   the ginormous itty bitty
a simple *beauty*, but such a dull word
in english; the latin *pulchritude* stiff as a
starched white collar – why not witness *hermoso*,
spanish makes it drift and linger

to breathe, in the light sweet darkness –
not the glare of daytime the shrink of

its heat; nor the bright pin and pierce
of a vision; no eulogising of celestial light
over the dark satanic   remember the brighter
than a thousand suns light the vandalic glow above
hiro-shima

i dream of the gnostic *pleroma*
before the light and dark fissure,
that superstitious rifting: eternal hymn
of the cicada hummingbird within latticed
weaves of the loose cosmic raft – *pleroma*,
foremost word of fullness; did the gnostics eat
grated carrot?

note

curious for proof of some danger
as you wait for a first glasses fitting
just touch the optician's hotplate your
fingertips burn quick as a whack from a
catapult is this the heat that they warn you is hell

look at the blisters blown up on your fingers
like bubbles extruding from gum, or pearly growths
you inspect on a plant, they shine in the light
of the chemists into milky beads
of a big rosary of glass

thread needles through the small tips
of your fingers admire the fineness of your skin
pale cotton praying on your hand you are taught
to kiss his bodily beauty in its suffering
you inscribe your own thank you notes

pilgriminal

pray shall we let us
for all our prayers in
the chapel of callous
elbows those discretionary
walkways of mortification
that pilliwinks can stay in
the toy box today
substantiational
the deep sawdust rug
masking an arcane forest
of worms, his tongue
was black as childhood

rung

i

behind the bathroom door
it endures the wasted years
covered in dust, draped in
an ancient sarong, its rungs
to hang disoriented clothes,
the defunct fish tank's plastic
pump upon; once or twice a year
dragged through the narrow doorway
for its clunky aid; the aluminium
clang does not approximate
brass bell jubilations chiming
a celestial throng: the mere
replacement of a light bulb,
perfunctory means to a domestic
end – whoever contemplates,
experiences the numinous in watts

ii

no way *the ladder* of perpetua –
vision of the martyr from carthage
(hannibal's progeny perhaps) who
climbed the 'golden ladder of marvellous
height' – avoiding swords, lances, hooks,
daggers fixed to its sides, and underneath
a crouching dragon of wondrous size – to reach

an immense garden at the top where a snow
haired shepherd was milking sheep while thousands
of white robed ones stood around; he gave her a gift
of a cake of cheese, so much sweeter than sara lee's;
this heaven a legend to compete with enid blyton's
'faraway tree'; staminade to endure those beasts and swords,
the rips and blows of her martyrdom: if i'd known all this
i'd have sat up straighter for sister perpetua and not sucked
on lifesavers during rosary

iii

great thorny branches of bougainvillea leap and lurch
towards the sky; junglegreen and purple riot in the air.
i try to prune them. cut them back into some kind of
order no topiary, after my father dies; his ladder is my
ladder now; so too the long thin arms of the cutters,
their blades curved like hungry beaks. a self-initiate i
climb the silver ladder on uneven ground underneath
the thick muscled animal that has wound itself round
the rotting wooden pergola that is the driveway
carport. i push and cut through gaps in the vines,
scratching my arms on the thorns, thinking of the war
in the pacific and new guinea, of my father on the
radio surveillance barge along its coast, of malaria and
love. sometimes the safety clips on the ladder's sides
almost slip but i take my chances in this driveway rite.
where i once stood in this green shade with my scooter
or skipping rope worrying over how much sin i'd

clocked up because my unwell mother hadn't taken me to sunday mass – sister augustine would interrogate next day. soon enough.

this ladder has no fine points sticking up towards heaven. i feel no drowse. no golden dream like after apple picking. i am tense with purpose on these cool metallic rungs. something urgent etches the moment. then comes the buzzing of the neighbours' children a fringe of leaves away. getting ready for their evening meal under the sukkoth shelter built in their garden for the feast of the tabernacle. i will gather up the thorny branches in the honeying dark's warm hum.

iv

ladder
            in a stocking
     rebel
            in the weave
                        hear the pages
                  ripple
                        in an opening book

v.

allegri's 'miserere': listen, the ladder curves to spiral, the voice's celestial rope; cool sparklings of the hyssop to assuage the greasy life; the cd spins a crystalline moment & someone sullen up above increases the

volume of clubland's sweaty mantras, the imperious
weight of an neighbourial thud –

vi

yeats knew the disloyalty of ladders
the vanishing of rungs in the windy spaces
of old minds; who end up after all those heady
moments back down on hands and knees across
familiar rubbled ground, small hearts picking through
the rags and bones of diminished time; jay gatsby who
saw a ladder forming through the pavement cracks one
starry american night forfeited this ascent, where
he could *romp like the mind of god*, discarded it for the
incarnate moment of a daisy-glittered kiss that shot him to
death flat on a pneumatic pool mattress, under a cold blown
sky; wittgenstein's ladder of language offers no placebos:
throw it away after use

the coloured ladder of juan miro, reaching up to an inky
nightsky in 'dog barking at the moon': a ladder to look at, too
bright to climb even just through your eyes, and the gap at the
top too narrow the width between rungs at the bottom too
wide – enjoy the image in a childhoodedly, a 'go-to-sleep'
poster sort of way, but his sculpture of a pitchfork tilting at the
sky is something to touch, to grip and grasp, to poke at all the
hangers on, daemonic vagrants in hovers throughout the sky

vii

why do we assume we must go *up* the ladder. some thralldom to medieval images of sinners falling down the ladder to hell and the lascivious instruments of satan's torturers. but subterranea holds more secrets, beauties than those of the dark deceiver. gold silver, all the gems. sapphires rubies emeralds amethysts ambers. their etheric magics. psyche's prophylactics. all the treasures of whoever's, whatever's creations stacked up and sleeping in time's (gaia's?) catacombs. cixous writes of her childhood experience of the story of jacob's ladder. how she was drawn to the images of descending angels. she writes of the dream ladder. going down. growing into the earth. the descent on the ladder of writing will be tough. down through the spirit body of flesh and earth.

but me. i look for an easier solution. enough of biblical endurance and ordealism. i climb down the ladder of memory. rusting, salty, white-painted rungs. the nervous thrill of that moment. not the tongue stretching up for the dry, sticky host of a first communion gravitas but arms reaching out for that first swim in deep water. letting go of gravity and pushing out into the glossy emerald waters. the heart electrified in the momentum of its liberation. sun streaming through squinted eyes. arms lifting over the water like sudden wings. kicking towards epiphany. so this is heaven.

contributory notes:–

i

poems in the little mags & journals
just seen & not heard in the long
insistences
of prose shadows flip the pages flip them back not the
street directory
for your city   you keep on getting lost in the colossal
end of prose town
(does it have a park –

who's been her own drip therapist   all these years   now
charity begins at home
admission rather than submission is the way   tee gee
stamped self addressed envelopes will
not be required   love your feral filing cabinet
like a free vacation

ii

love me love my ancient beach towel
poems suspended in its salty nap the third eye's
lint spins like a mirror ball as a wet brow hits
mancunian sand   you follow the
mermaid down the breathing chambers
of emerald cream then
a voice from new year 1963 distracts you
that mexican jockey sitting in your lap crooning

something forgettable & not love letters
in the sand
this shard of solar memorabilia
trivial as a paddle pop stick
laughs through your veins like an
amateur lyric so who wants to be professional

iii

is god a professional with an embossed
business card
or is his business too big for that or
just too messy all over the place
let it rip that's how it happens anyroad
particle waving all through the universe inside & out
please imagine that yes sir that's my goddy
genderless & benderfull everywhere & nowhere
riding that beach towel right over the apocalypse
waving never drowning surviving in the breath of an
apple
ash of a volcano
lust of an iceberg
ye old black and white tv
irresistible & indivisible less than this is
ludicrous portrait galleries of fleshed out deities &
their messiahs
smell like batblown caves for nervy minds

iv

see how a poem's unwritten particles
swarm   to swim beyond flattening
nets of time

spoilt

i

there were no words to explain why
he looked but he did and the rest
is myth, version after version; through
the cypresses and pines of gargaphie
valley he sped like a hound her silvergold
wires tugged at his head in the midday
heat he could smell her ichorian blood –
into the gap the gape of his gaze she
flung water drops from her bathing pool,
with his feverish eye he had pierced her
fierce naked seclusion, overreached
his mortal limits; a goddess is a goddess did
he forget, his moment was over before it began
as the stag horns pushed up through his forehead
his new animal body, meaty spoils for his fifty hounds
and their bellies, the hunter soon devoured, and scattered
for aeons

ii

gazing at the divine
with too much gasping for
sacred propinquity, does
this spoil, damage what is called
human; imploratory thrusts of the self
towards sculptures, statues, shrines,

paintings, cards, frescoes, beads – the
iconopathic: fresh phanic desire curdling
into debris sentimental; are we alone on
the earth to comprehend being, finite
and little –

nog

namaste to the nameless
& the dateless holiday appears

you are wasting time sending
your current god a jubilation

postcard do you think any sort
of god would need a stamp

a god with an address: broken wing
dysfunctional handbag stale meringue

step out of your name & let it
splutter on the sand hear the wind

speed your portafiled history to the shipwreck
of the 'dies irae' the seas comb filaments

of hair for new animations every day
vacational in the pink shell cake

soft hoods of saints

wolf

a small magazine its bright yellow cover. shiny. cute as a book. black and white comic awaiting young readers in the penultimate pages. a new virgin martyr. this saint. her thick story. too much black ink in the artist's bodies and words. this young girl who resisted her attacker, the room whispers *rape*. the slash stab of his knife raised in the air like a raged eye of a prophet, his hair slick as a fifties film star. this tale of the holy maria goretti to stalk young girl catholics; would it scare them so quietly they might even laugh. a subscription to 'harvest' was almost compulsory, like the perfect girl who would always choose death.

make up

forty years as a maid
to the fatinellis of lucca
tuscany still gave zita
a ton of time to become
a saint she couldn't help
herself she just had to help
the poor: leave bread baking
in the oven when off on a charity
call give away the family bean stores
in a famine give her master's fur cloak
to a beggar at the door

                                    & the bread's watched over
by a bunch of angels found in the kitchen
(maybe they were hungry too) the cupboard full
of beans again an angel moonlighting as a beggar
returns the fur cloak next day – holy card zita holds
the cloak in her hand, white with black flecks, ermine

– maybe brigitte bardot wouldn't like this card but would
zita like b. bardot; zita was bolder than a sex kitten
bolder than the brass of a church   saints are a part of
celebrity but who would pray to a movie star primping on
in a make up van, enduring the stare of a thicker light,
fussing over heightcellulite & snapping only a good side;

like domestic servants and maids stars could pray to
zita – as a finder of lost keys, i don't know how she got
this additional gift, perhaps there's an upgrade degree
for saints like her : how to deal with a swipe keycard

liquiddity

the five foot nun, named after a benedictine monk,
who saved st placid from drowning in the dictionary
of saints. here she is, gripping her pragmatic grace,
that ample teapot, in a photo blown up to mural size
on the hospital's foyer wall   *caritas christi urget nos*
                                        pouring tea into cups with
saucers held by men in faded hats and suits   they
called them euphoniously 'vagrants' then   close
to the bottom of the cliff face wall: car park to
indifferent naval vehicles today   through the
photographic black and white a smell of ancient
patience in the sandstone layers of the rock   i know
her face i like it   i liked it forty fifty years ago

fresh presentness of time   spreads like unexpected
honey   *hello* she used to say eye to eye the
full blackness of her habit passing through the
passageway between the refectory and the convent,
home to retired and working nuns sprightly alert
elderly and just a little amused and pleased   past
chirping girls in the junior school yard   bags of
coke stacked at the rear for the laundry fires   *hello*

next to the renovated information desk i stare at
her steaming offerings in quiet surmise   here in
another century   perfect and so carefully plain

invitation

some saints' lives make good stories
and good pictures especially if
the supernatural elements look crisp
and impressive on paper or whatever;
i am sitting here flipping through book
iii of miniature stories of saints copyright
1946, a little book of boy saints   i pass
augustine, christopher, greg the great,
stanislaus whose name i always liked,
sebastian, too fetishised by now, and stop
for a break at robert the white monk, an
english cistercian, sitting in profile at a small
table near a window; he wears a modest halo,
this long-boned monk, big raised eyes his skin
blueish pink one hand on his contemplative
brow; two small pieces of bread (though they
look like chipolatas) from a cut loaf lie on the table
and a crucifix sits firm on the wall behind – what holds
me to this page is the image of a golden plate suspended
in the air outside the window its bright aura spreading out
above the trees and the long winding road like theophanic
margarine or a mid-twentieth century ufo – looking at this
picture makes my ears ring – and i read of how the day before
robert gave his bread and honey to a poor man he saw through
the window and hey presto the next day this plate appeared the

monks knew this was christ himself another version speaks of buttered oatcake and the stranger as an angel

it is said that on his death bed robert's soul was seen ascending to heaven like a ball of fire that he is depicted in art holding a church his spartan eating habits sure didn't make him weak. unfortunately there was a bit of a downsize to the myth of robert not included in the picture book. but saint bernard of clairvaux whom robert visited, dismissed as slander the story of robert's relations with a pious woman and gave robert a girdle for performing cures. a miracle linked to robert is the wellbeing of a monk who fell unhurt from a ladder while whitewashing the dorm.

when i was a catholic i didn't know of this
robert but i have a fondness for him now
i know him although that's not really true
it is the picture of the gold plate out the window
that i like it's got a grip on me especially when i see
emily dickinson also clothed in white walking down
the road below the plate, from her nature's dining room

wool

to weave three baskets daily
in exchange for enough bread and
vegetable to stay just fed, warm
craft of prayer not chilled penances –
corpus humanus stretching up the
desert mountains, rocks, wading
through the sands like glowing skeletons
the sapphiric fire the deep orange
octagonals of their hearts the song
of the nimbus radiant in the cold
egyptian nights, fathers of the desert
anchorite eyes pulling upwards like curled
determined feet on ropes from grubby caves
towards the golden ships of heaven years
and years and years of this, rejecting all the talk
and hector of the stoa to engage divinity inside
the state of hesychia, and so reach apatheia –

who noticed the old smashed skulls
of newborn lambs scattered, uncovered
on the ground after a plague of sandstorms,
in a ring like a broken rosary: *by these bones*
would you not know me

shiny

lovely rita of cascia from the fifteenth century, saint of impossible causes; rita kneeling at the cross in her nun's cell at the augustinian monastery, with the ray of light on the holy card pouring down on the wound on her forehead from her crown of thorns; rita and her passion for the passion of christ; rita and her festering wound that wouldn't heal for years, until the occasion of her death when the wound's worms transformed into twinkling lights shining like rubies in the now perfumed air; pope john paul the second in a talk on humility and obedience to commemorate one hundred years of her canonisation, announces on the twentieth of may of the year two thousand anno domini that this 'shiny mark' is 'a verification of her christian maturity'

rita and the miracle healings at her tomb,
and beside her deceased body on its catafalque
in fourteen fifty seven – paralysis evil spirits
blindness; rita who survived marital violence
to enter the monastery at the age of thirty six
for a long holy life immersed in the adoration
of wounds and suffering; rita baby rita little
honey bun five days old and visited by a swarm
of white bees after her baptism buzzing bees

surrounding her tiny face entering her mouth
with no damage done; rita of the impossible
receiving a rose from a bush at roccaporena
in her last winter when roses never bloom –
flamboyant rita: your pink hagiography your
perfumaria, where are you now

spring or autumn of nineteen fifty seven or eight: a group of twelve year old catholic school girls is attending an open day at the ave maria retreat house in sydney's point piper, with its view of the harbour. this grandeur of god. but the view in the cloisters goes deeper. they creep up the narrow spiral stairs to a cell. there on the pillow lies a wooden replica of the crown of thorns. o rose art thou sick. the shock of this witness to the worship of cruelty resounds like a poem beautiful stains of saints on the ground. the pulchritude of enduring pain. smashed fruit lying there across the wayside. the god delirium. red orange purple trickles of the soul. hard stones of faith and forbearance remain after the pain has dried.

adalbert adelaide agape agatha amadour apollonia asaph attracta
bathild bavo benignus blaise blandina botolph bona of pisa
carpus chad chrodegang chrysogonus cloud cuby

glistening white dumplings. a sunday yum cha communion. the mouth plump with indulgence. but isn't this god's creation. the pack of holy cards you purchase later. how the saints float above the paper in the steamy ginger ether.

dyfrig dympna edburga eligius erconwald ethelburga of barking
eulalia eulogius euphemia evurtius eystein
fabiola fiacre frideswide fructuosus frumentius fulgentius fursey

souls popping up like convenience stores in every necessary country. hundreds of new saints. more than all his predecessors created since fifteen eighty eight. we know what he was thinking of. john paul's restoration project. fortifying church pillars against the chisels of the western cynics. the finest forged steel on god's planet. big parcels of food dropped from divine rescue planes. bellies burp with legenda. sweet haloes of saints. the descent of bright iced donuts.

and all those journeyman saints. over a thousand hanging onto the lower rungs of beatification. hanging on for that extra canonising miracle. our australasian ladies in waiting, aubert of new zealand, mackillop of north sydney. not lucrative enough for rome. the low population of the antipodes not worth the politics. the hagiographic haggle. a laconic clientele.

gall godelive godric hedwig hilarion hildegard homobonus illtyd januarius jarlath john john john john john climacus

don't we love the stories of saints' lives. well some of them. not the hordes haloed for building up the monastries of the medieval church. god's good bureaucrats. but the magican saints. the showbiz circus sideshow, the special effects saints. the stars.

saints who survived fire. arrows. starvation. fasting. stigmata bleeding. bilocation saints. all the miracle healer saints. decapitated saints who created fresh springs of water in the spot their heads fell. performance artists multiplying the scripts of god.

kentigern (or mungo) leger liberata ludger lull lutgard
macarius the elder macrina the younger mamas mary mary mary méen
mildburga norbert notburga odilia omer otto

saints show us who we aren't. impossible to imitate. our prayers too fast. impatient. saints and their trust in their god. slow and endless. wearing belief like soft hoods. invisible protective. we can only gawk at their images, legenda. in the holy cards many saints are accompanied by floral arrangements. flowers. do saints have flaws. once they are officially saints surely all flaws must hit the floor to be swept away in the giant hagionic broom.

pammachius pancras pantaleon peter peter peter philibert
polycarp peter & peter
radegund raineld rhipsime rock rupert
scholastica senan of scattery symphorian the seven sleepers

in heaven how many saints envy each other's feats. do they respect each other in the bright immensity of their habitats. do they reach halo fatigue.

theodore the studite tiburtius uncumber victricius
walburga willehad willibald winwaloe wenzel

saints usually look too beautiful in the artworks. on the cards. their colours. the tilt of their heads. their limpid eyes. you like to stroke the smoothness of their ethery cloaked limbs with your thoughts. why not imagine them as spiritual pets.

streamers

streamers

a series of koannes

weigh the rice before you boil it
how else can you catch up
with yourself wash the radish
after you eat it the soil requests
you share its emergency although its
colour may not suit your hand towel

when the lounge begins to sound like you
you will know you have walked far
enough; how the cupboards open
their doors as the shower deliberates

a choice of empty restaurants
a shudder of tree fern harvests
in your bitter hair

breakfast emotion the
red cup predestined
for its own duchy,
could the venison sestina
take you to hell and back
oyster shell serf

syrup of heaven
why gloss over a
terrazzo confessional
while the moon's been
requisitioned

white chalk dust swathes
across the mirror the manual
defuncts; scribes of the mountain
polish their eyeballs with
several ideas

the dream dog barks
mid-caninese and you
bark back in spanglish in
the neighbour's dream you yell
in caesarine no river
to cool your salmon

the wedding dress
bakes on the roof
of the grass soup arcade
the visa has broken its zipper
the key ring escapes to the noodle
farm who will gut the fish for
its funeral

a caravan, patient where
a gate once stood dusty as
a parable; a used match floats
in a toilet bowl confident
as a petal

which tooth was
a legal witness to
the desecration of
the costume jewel
the treasonable sonnet
intended a wiser jaw
but the sunrise was
so ugly that era

so the rabbit mistakes
the walking stick for
a chocolate carrot: clouds
reject elision

the zoom of the red bee
speeding through the bedroom
mad sportscar lost in the dunes
the voltaire biography lies on the
pillows with its barcode visible how
many chances do we get

rinse the grain from
your woolworth's bowl
have you nothing
better to do with it paddle
pop sticks have made
good wallets

may the glass floor give you
more life span; opportunity
in the buried city arrives in
the corazon hour are you metric
or imperially inclined

yesterday you lived
forever all the paper
shone as if the air was round
today the dumpling wears
a frown the news disturbs old
sand

leave the words
in the family crypt
and hurry to the shallow
sea before the siren instills
a false alarm; paddle
before you tread
curtains of dread
boot heavy hung
on hooks to impede,
the violence of furniture
the domestic insult can
you respect their colour
their oligarchic weight
where will it lead this
morning

you miss the bus
before it arrives how easy
to change the light bulb

the window shutters
glow of another morning
what a pity the shade's
revarnish

a harvest of worries
which barn to store them
before the termites gather –
the spoon stirrer loses sight
of the spoon

how not to be surprised
by a surprise, see how
the day has no waistline
how the vovo is not
in the constitution how
the words did not add
up how ordinary it is
to turn the page

birdsong collides
with the motor industry
above the breakfast grain
the four wheels of sunset
streak the sky

can it ever be known
what the carpet knows
the shoe too wet
with the world the ear
so itchy with fish

the still violence
sprawls on the hard
floor the prongs of its
plug clench at the point
of its power there are numerous
options for paying the next bill;
the forest it brushes your heart

small opinions for
the handy life grab
all the stainless steel
in sight bone dry
the mural's imbrications
finesse the roll of a blank
dice

the song yearns
in the lachrymose
room chiffon a
dubious collateral
the ceiling no placebo
& punctuation scattering
in the rayon's whistle

taking the memory
for a walk like a hat
that needs defustering
the driftwood sails at
dawn the lay-by docket
was never enough; lids
dip in the mirror's ledger
wakame is the new lover

the sand tolerates its own
forgetfulness; patiently it
waits for us to recall a smell
of footsteps – what language
does the buried icecream
wrapper offer

between the clouds
the litter of dialogue
an abuse of pronouns
let the white drift across
with no view in sight
wind of euphoria is
plain enough

the missing trail of
breadcrumbs has left
nothing to the imagination
no way to track it down in
the belly of a bird and the kitchen
in a swelter, the hunger in its barren
cupboards barely a statistic

amphora

she kept her distance

she kept her distance in a yellow and blue lacquered box she had bought on dal lake. she arranged the box on top of the mauve trunk from shepherd's bush markets, next to a book on the history of walking and virgil's georgics and eclogues; alongside a slim silver torch.

she kept her distance close to her ribs like a favorite ghost more real than the squeak of the windows being lifted to acknowledge another day.

she protected this distance in the summer by closing the windows against the predations of wasps which would fly in and circle it as soon as the sun was strong.

she felt so reassured by the mutual tutelage between herself and her distance she could float through numerous walls, disappointment a long way off.

counter

the trouble with leaving things up in the air is that they can become hard to find. good intentions, arrangements for coffee, dental appointments, ideas for a poem. a sky of maybes. on one occasion i looked for them with opera glasses. unsuccessfully. it's not as though the air is full of shelves, as far as i know. though that's not very far. you might look up into the air and see nothing much. there's a lot of space up there. you look up and your mouth goes o-o-o like a series of small balloons. perhaps if a coffee cup saucer came flying through the air towards you you might suddenly recall what it was you had left up there. some people leave their lives up there in the air. they feel that way it's easier to survive if they don't have a life and especially if they're always being pestered to get one. it's simpler just to exist. breathe away. in out round about. let your life drift out of sight. it's not really perdition, but a sub-branch of pragmatism.

what puzzles me is how people get up in the air, to be able to leave anything there. material technology can be expensive. christine the astonishing, according to thomas of cantimpré, could make herself light as a bird. she could stay up in the air perched on the smallest of twigs. she could also remain under water for ages, this saint christine. six days for example. but would you want to leave anything under the water that long. she's pretty impressive. especially her exemplary suffering. and she's not hard to find. she's up there on the top shelf of penguin classics. just leave your bag at the counter.

escort

they walk on it drop matter on it sleep on it assemble furniture on it vacuum wash polish it. with the usual appliances. despite its occult provenance even a broom is an appliance. most people have a matter of fact relationship with the floor.

but there are propitious people. people you can wipe the floor with. people who reach out with their hands and instruct you to escort them over across and around your floors with your eyes closed. people whose lustrous skin can only be imagined. skins that burnish, refine your floors till they have no gravity. fine as a wish.

subjunctive

choice is always there. leave the diary pages blank. write down nothing. admire the big white pages. blank after blank. you can call this openness freedom. turn the gold edged pages. january march june october – this luxury of pretending you have nothing you need to remember to do. could you be this reckless.

choice is always there. stack the day like a giant warehouse of time capital. stretch the day. divide it into hours half hours quarter hours minutes. fill each diary timeslot with intentions plans activities meetings. divide the time into shorter and shorter units. time is so generous so amenable to portioning. and so overbearing. you are now overloaded with chronology. will you regret this aggrandisement.

——

she knew it was time to move on. leave the diary to its interrogative covers. she slid onto her feet into the ebony dark of the longest night of the year, crossed the highway, and began her run through the lure of the city's traffic tunnels designed to save time. she ran and she ran and she ran, like a digital marathon princess swathed in fresh plasma. might

she run out of breath as she ran through and out
of time towards the edge of the athanasian plains.
there in their thereness. in such blasé glory.

she wasn't to be found in the list. his eyes darted down the long line of the 'c's : chevron barracuda chimaera cigar wrasse clown toby comet convict surgeon fish coronation cod. he even ventured into the 'd's in case she had become a fugitive reluctant to be lured into giving her piscine blessing. but she wasn't hiding behind the dash dot goat fish glowing in the screen's sheen. he was becoming frustrated by this expedition at the cheapest internet café on the strip. the connection was slow and the air-con shabby. there was no surfing here, more like weekend fishing. still he had plenty of time to find her, the fish of his dreams, to mount on his neon peach wall of digital print out pinups in his three star caravan 'lorelee'. gilbert, single since his engagement party in the local park the month sergeant peppers lonely hearts club band was released, had to find this latest fish whose silky form had brushed against his eyelids in his best dream hours between four and five am, whispering like dolly parton 'my name is *compliment* and there's plenty of me'.

incubator

funny to see all those green plastic bags lined up in the hot steamy street like rejection's incubator. the word 'glad' stamped on them. would you want to peep inside. perhaps they contain a few of someone's old glad rags. sad sacks. but he was a comic not a sack. his military uniform looked neat enough though his civvies could look a little shabby. i guessed his body sagged. maybe the sack referred to bags under his eyes. sac seems the better word form.

why do we speak of clothes as glad rags. rags always look a little melancholic. depressed. why would you want to go out on the town in rags. who'd have you. you'd be feeling far from glad. unless you're part of the cutting edge and want to pout about in the recession look. repressing your gladness until the cocktail hour. absinthe and sprite.

the methylated rag for cleaning glass. how glad is that. when the word window shines. do we want ours opaque.

glad rags in a glad bag. perhaps they're on the way to a charity bin. a word wears well. happy to be given away. relocated. pre-loved yet post-forgotten.

cup

phrases of time prowl through the language. you need to be on your guard. what's the time mister wolf. a game we used to play as children. how far could we goad mister wolf till he would chase and grab us. just as he tried to grab red riding hood. like mister wolf whose belly was his timepiece, time has its own sharp teeth. i know. i nearly bled to death in the nick of time.

one winter morning as i reached out to turn off my alarm clock and have forty five more winks i felt a little jab on the inside of my wrist. i didn't think too much about it. my body often quarrels with itself when in sleep. an unexplained bruise, a small serration. red dots dawn on me in the mirror when i finally rise. me levanto. a good verb, the spanish for getting up. all floaty and transcendent. lifting you above the mortal, time's gridded plane.

who knows how long forty five winks really are. we think we can gauge forty winks reasonably well. but that extra five could last for hours. sleep can stretch as well as shrink time. as i slept i sensed the sheet getting sticky. one side of my body felt very heavy, one felt light. a six cup white electric jug came into view. the gauge showed only three cups of my blood remained. i was startled. i lifted up the lighter of my arms and saw blood dripping down from that small incision in my wrist that i had ignored. what had done this to me. surely the jagged edge of my plastic alarm clock couldn't be that vicious.

the helicopter's rotor blades thwacked and juddered across the sky. it was coming closer. probably one of the naval exercises you get round here. or terrorist watch rehearsal time. time's winged chariot hurrying too near. i shot up from the pillows. the jab mark was still there. but the sheets were dry. how intimate is the relationship between the nick of time and the eye of a needle. it would take me a while to find out. i had been sleeping on my glasses.

lucky dip

it was more than food for thought and less than unpleasant. for years i had wanted to own one. i had a liking for the genuine article since i'd seen them in all those movies of intrigue in the tropics. the one i finally purchased years later wasn't cheap, although it was generic and very conveniently packed in a cylinder. for easy storage and transportation. there was something about the way it was rolled tight in a wavelike shape. something that reminded me of pringles. the idea took hold of me like a huge joke. and i just had to try it. perhaps it was a little reckless but ever since i was a small child i'd been fascinated by the story of a boy i knew who'd swallowed money and then had to eat cotton wool sandwiches to ease its way through his intestinal system. he had grown up to be a celebrated marine geologist so it can't have done him any harm.

i went to the fridge to inspect my current stock of dips, half a dozen or so in various stages of maturity. after checking the dates on their lids i decided on four: guacamole, moroccan, chilli crab, and tzatziki. i carefully cut the right side into small pieces trying to keep as close as possible to the pringles shape, and slid them into the various dips. unlike the originals they didn't seem to snap in the dipping. swallowing was pretty simple. they seemed to glide down my alimentary canal like tiny rafts, aided on their downward path by a modicum of wind. as for what remained of it i turned it upside down and filled it up with bird seed and left it to its own devices under a tree. the foil i had used to replace the consumed right side made it glint like a lunar attraction; with some of the seed spilt along what was left of the brim, mimicking the shape of a littoral.

quite a passive aggrandisement. let life grow those soft goods for you. while you read the wallpaper's stories. what a secret library goes unnoticed. this intramural privacy is your good fortune. your imagination plumes with the energy of sails.

only once every six weeks you face travail. embark on your collection tour in your pick-up truck. you load the dozens of pails of dust from the inner and outer fields of your farm *debris* (named after a sacred river) into the tray, snap down the covers and transport the harvest to your warehouse where it is packed into the waiting magazines. you tamp your dust crop down into these huge clay storage containers shaped like giant amphoras. you do it from a love of the substantial. this reliable process year after year. when there are enough of these dust petrifications to create a triumphal avenue of columns you will smash open the clay and complete your architectural plan. there you will recline in your best dust jacket (the wallpaper now a faded entertainment, a resource for the songbooks of bugs) and browse the dharma of dust whisperings while playing the harmonium at auspicious interludes of mist.

relief

retirement-age you asks for the slip which lists the classes to relief teach for the day. before he has time to hand it to you the other one standing in the office for a natter speaks in a smirk of a 'petticoat'. god. what a dag. those pale grey shoes should have been an indication. he wouldn't know you discarded slips about forty years ago. the smell of that old school chalk. how time slips away but the smell doesn't. smell of your teenage slip singeing after you wrapped it round your bedlamp late at night on a school day, anxious to conceal your awakeness from your mother while you devour 'the portrait of dorian gray'. giving the gods of reading lust the slip as a burnt offering. that added sweat of a slip over pantyhose. the purple stain from the fordigraph spirit duplicator on your new-teacher cream linen skirt. for the friday morning spelling list and the revision of participial phrases. heatwave sweat coated with chalk dust, flies, the drought. dry hills of a country school. they used to say you're snowing down south if your half petticoat slipped. you gave it the slip alright. flew away through the slipstream. slipped through history to a dream of temples ruined palaces the blue imagination of a broken column tripped over in the grass. slip of ancient shadows across the heart. zipped into the spirit of denim. rusted on you like a reckoning. you slipped through a cordoned off area at knossos to touch a wisp of original fresco with a determined lip.

pogo

lathe

it's always seemed a marshmallow word
'poppet' a kind of sloppy kiss word, sounding
alert but soft in affect: 'my little poppet'; those
plastic beads of the fifties & sixties teenage girls could
make up their own necklaces and bracelets from
poppets, one bead's round pin fitting into the next
one's hole a sublimated copulation chain proteins have
been described as a chain of amino acids strung
together like poppet beads and the comic novelist
who commented on the popularity of his lectures on tess
of the d'urbervilles to undergraduates at sydney university
in the sixties said in an interview that in his youth he packed
poppet beads for his family's business, thirty poppets a necklace;
wikipedia informs that poppet dolls are fertility symbols and
can be made of fruit, corn shafts, potato, that poppet dolls can
be used for 'magick'; poppets also feature in the lexicon of ships
and lathes, the technology of objects not the craft of demonology;
in arthur miller's crucible a poppet doll with a needle stuck
in its belly is discovered in the home of elizabeth proctor
after abigail is found screaming with a needle in her guts
screaming loud enough to make a bull weep says cheever
– was it rosary beads that lizzy proctor the good puritan needed
in the aftermath she certainly got shafted, ring a ring a rosey a
pocketful of posey, can poppets make good rosary beads may
the polysemic flower

the twitch quartet

i vita minora

not a poet to lyricise on fruit
i used to throw my school lunch orange
into the smelly bin how i loved to hear
that thud a continental frankfurt was
more my thingumajig but a word's
vibration can surprise the mouth's
demands, so it was in the breakfast
room of frankfurt's monopol hotel
when i looked at the fruits displayed
'pflaumen' inscribed on a little placard
in front of the bowl of stewed plums –
well the fruit was in fact fairly delicious
but it was 'pflaumen' that made my throat
feel more like 'delirious'; the ripple and flow
of the 'pfl' and the long slow glide of the vowels
through 'm', dipping an oar in the water by
the shade of a willow, a breeze on a saucer
of cream; better than williams wc's filching of
plums from that new jersey fridge i could go
back and back for more with no forgiveness
needed; to speak with a plum in the mouth though
is no sensory treat down in the antipodes, more of
an old world impediment, but who couldn't wouldn't
lie down in a soft bed of pflaumen; even if that mouthful
of plum has come from the prunus genus; not every plum

is a plum is a seductive pflaume the ancients built their fierce walls of plums, giant stones named after the cyclops, one hundred pounds or more each one you can inspect them at the citadel of tiryns – but all the fortification i can offer you right now is a sip of old plum brandy

ii still life minus puffed cream

mademoiselle lupin stressed out french teacher
at cliff house school great britain circa late
nineteen forties thinks bessie bunter's failure
in oral translation is due to a mouth full
of apple; when bessie insists she's eating
a *pear* mademoiselle is totally enraged; a *pear*
a *pear* bessie reinsists to lupin whose nose tip
turns burgundy: you have a *pair* of apples,
two!– linguistic grace descends in the form of
classmate babs : une *poire* mam'selle, c'est
une *poire*   these juicy homonympish moments
as bessie forfeits half holiday

iii stew

how did the animated 'ginger' get caught up with
word on a budget 'gingerly', this spicy rhizome
from the genus zingiber – through medieval french
old english to latin greek originally prakrit thanks
macquarie dick, the greek version really had a zip
'zingiberis' an aromatic word, zephyr with a lift;
'gingerly' s a violation of the root so wary dull and

cautious : she took the packet of arrowroot biscuits
off the shelf as gingerly as she could; if 'gingerly'
derives from the comparative of 'gent', noble and
graceful as in old french, how come 'to ginger' is a
working verb for a prostitute thieving from a client's
clothes; ginger anything still tastes good – cake wine
stirfry noodle stew except when you're clogged up with flu

iv crush

cold glasses of thick cherry juice
in oranienburgerstrasse berlin,
you could soar on a bladder full
of kirsche saft, amrita of the earth
kirsche – only an 's' between it and
kirche, the serpentine 's' not as refreshing
in a church, ssss-h mary's barefoot on that
serpent's head, no wine pressing here,
no satan saft; kirche, church – something too
blunt in the texture; so what about église,
there's a word to gloat on, the glint and glister
of a glacé fruit: this is a word and here's its
steeple, raise the paten and just watch the people

oh

'tuross' was the name
of my family home the plate
obscured by branches of a hedge
as if there were no pride in the name,
or simply indifference 'tuross' was just 'tuross';
being this morning in a semantic state of mind
– and a romantic one, wishing 'tuross' to be a
scottish hero a rob roy leaping through the heather
with his sword glinting – i googled 'tuross' ; all i got
were holiday and fishing sites in new south wales –
i want a 'tuross' that feels a little more robust i don't
want an antipodean holiday or an angling travel guide,
or a let down – like that visit from the man from porlock
who interrupted coleridge from kubla khan; still, this
person from porlock could have been a disguised visitor
from parnassus sent to impede coleridge from flooding
his verse for the worse and drowning in his words, and
not some mundane business pest, like a notary's
emissary; stevie smith saw this person from porlock as
a positive arrival at chez sam – she'd have liked her own
porlock person to quieten her thoughts; at least the man
from porlock got into the history of poetry, better known
than the man from snowy river   is 'porlock' a place
name like 'tuross', a name with an information block,
probably not; xanadu doesn't have this problem it
shimmers through pleasure's centuries

‘prufrock’ – now here’s a name that’s been upgraded
by the good old thomas stearns, a celebrated tragic
comic crooner, a balding orpheus; once merely the
name of a furniture store in his master’s home town of
saint louis: meet me at prufrock’s for a new sideboard
or a suite of dining chairs, staid and prudent what a
shock, not quite the place to purchase an analyst’s
couch –

tuross, porlock, prufrock: frissons in the vowel chain;
could an angling holiday in tuross bring in a big word
catch   *tu brute* *tu ross*

spreadsheet

does a collection of coasters have
more going for it than a collection
of blotters, something i used to collect
with temporary passion at every easter
show before the dispensation of the biro
pen; the banks were especially generous
with those stacks of giveaway blotters
for eager schoolkids to flash at each
other after easter as if gold
stars – the banking sector's diligence in
training the next generation of customers
(no investors then)
to take due care of their copybooks, free
blotters to absorb/avoid the blotting of
a copybook, a dictation, a composition
test, irony deeper than an inky
metal nib – a coaster

hints at an atmospheric levity, an intoxicating whiff
a hospitable aid for
the potentially blotto if their beer froth
should
overflow and
spill or the rings of cool
wine or shandy glasses make moist
imprints
on a table top, the coaster as decorum's

talisman; these aids to keep the land of
tables dry   why were they named coasters:
from some repressed domestic fear
of the sea's power ocean waves
spilling across dry sand
wetting shoes skirts frocks trouser legs   or slacks
spoiling that human furniture how
beer breaks over
a rim in waves   water
water everywhere   hormonal
stain adrenals of the sea
must be restrained
in convivial company –

roller coaster gives the word
more muscle
and more spunk   the giant wave machinery
curving up
and down the sky
how
the body's orifices scream
as they rise and fall
in gulps
of air   an orgy of the mechanical sublime
the popularity of risk   do all sleep sated unfrustrated
soundly in dry sheets

she's coasting along now the word edges
towards bad form neither wild or tamed a *tut tut tut*
travelling towards
that beach of indolence sand sea cerulean sky
no sawing through study's dark forests hammering logs
into tough little cabins of knowledge *they coasted all*
through high school university

here's five metal coasters decorated with postal art
a galore of stamps from around
the world –
cameroun belgian congo bolivia
chile australia israel germany france australia hungary
anywhere laos and great brit close one eye and spin the
coaster like a globe lots of fauna flora famous folks usa
nz canada kings and queens of course have a look at the
coronation of nineteen twenty three
great for the armchair
barstool traveller sipping on a pilsener pimms a gin or two
another
another nostalgia cocktail where's that old
album the yellowed hinges clinging onto a
confectionery of stamps that wizzed you
through a suburban bungalow's walls
to diverse mysteries

i chug along in my inner coastal trader
(how as a child one

would so swap stamps)
the jewel in this metallic stamp
collection: the hellenic one
the flower narcissus
and its eponymous boy
gazing forever into the pool
those stamps on the coasters echo
all those philatelic myths
spilling over the bubbling heart's
borderland

stock

always dicey, this word play. you let the words roll around in your mouth till their sheer brio pushes them out through your cheeks. qualmlessly. how long should the cud be chewn. chawn is a better word. but you hear the purists chut-chutting. the edges of words cutting.

you dice the vegetables like a textbook illustration. neat and uniform in a flourish of neo-housewifely earnestness. and then you realise your analogy is dicey. not nicey. you should have said the *gender neutral* 'cook'. you are dicing on the cutting board for a stockpot or stew. be careful with the spelling. a stewe is out of favour here. though for flavour a few more cloves of garlic and a sprig of rosemary may be required. and if a visitor is coming ask them to bring some dried shrimp and raw prawn. something fishy. in case you change your mind and make a broth.

take a cup of dice
and throw, less control
over the ingredients now, they
roll out as they please: firm

white dots like the eyes of
potatoes, eyes of a god of chance,
(maybe the potato one) tweaking fates
as the numbers fall, from a levitational
couch
    stock cube   parsnip cube   dice cube
        do chefs take such gambols

here is one dice lost
behind a scratched chair leg
change the word to 'die', dice
in the singular – bad luck to
roll just one; add a letter
and the gods reappear – 'dies',
they're never far away – waiting
to be fed, again and again

a toss of the salad is a more
pragmatic option (though less
pain, less gain): 'dice' an imperative
in latin – so say it, fortune
teller, spill the beans

writing in the dark

nocturnal emission

the mouth fills with land
after midnight it's hard
to understand if you're
not there at the wharf
it might take some stretch
of the imagination you walk
off the water with your mouth
wide open and new countries rush
to fill it, a tongue identifies them
(diviner chef fleece classer, badges
of a history of taste):

providence, nocturnal
providore, a geography
of faith, when you swallow you
don't choke on a wild herb's lotion

eheu fugaces

for miles (as far as a child
could see) the night city curved
around the sky, a handsome
platter, comfortable and ignorant
of its impositions, sequined in
monogrammed electro-light,
the black sky immersed in
its dark lullaby; too soon
the city obese with bright
light in a coup of fear, or
pontification, the sky filched
of its deep subtle bunks

shed

the offer of the dark tooth its
sudden sunlight a mouth so distant
from the derelict mirror the shrill
bleach of wind; night falls like dawn
a tongue shimmers in its polished garden
you touch it as it flees

news hour

take a walk through the sky windows
dark as books beyond the reach of
the usual scarf of motives how the red
lamp soars, its coal interior a passionate
revival in spite of the capitulation of ash and
those magnetic oaths the tower simmers as it leans backwards
into the emerald shadow the ticker tape fraying the memory
all its sorrow

this week next week
the week after

zag

the poems are running
running away running from
that dread of having to explain
themselves, those lists of
food ingredients they've
read on the back of packets
instant noodles for example;
they don't want to be registered
for gst or voting rights they know
they don't live in a democracy but
at least they can live in privacy if
they scatter

decorum

making room
in the room where
space is in its conceptual
phase: always room for more room
you are surprised how little space a body takes up
& the air a great host how a ledge of birdsong amplifies the book
of the room: epic wheeling across the ambient ceiling stoic
wall inhalation the paper of words: make believe lives, like a
life: survival minutiae & the carpet wove so deep with rumour

park

what is the theme of the theme
not quite the same as having two blue
balloons could there be the balloon of the balloon;
each balloon is separate and can be identical
(sort of – if two different persons blew them up
they would not be filled with the same air necessarily)
but unlike themes these balloons are not hierarchical:
the theme of the theme must be a broader theme so
if the theme of the festival is anger the theme of this
theme might be *emotion* or even bigger: *human behaviour* –
many people who attend the festival are in fact calm
personalities until they are told to prick the opening
night balloons released from the tower above the fifty
first level – is that a theme or a great idea: you might
have to beg the concept team for closure here

harvest

somewhere in tomorrow's living
room a puddle of blood designed as
a table of memory shining like pvc
in all its surface glory the veins of
domestic beatitudes open to a spring
shower and the cowskin rug cooing
like global pathology and those floral bruises

torch

i didn't get to the gutenberg
museum but i bought the book i
thought about going to ground
but i lacked a coffin or a headtorch
and had insufficient training in calling
a spade a spade the handicraft club was
sewing an auction across the particular
parcel i had inspected i did hear someone say
the hospital had been airlifted to another
kerbside but poets were surprisingly competent
people and anyhow the banyan tree over there by the
missing river would have enough remedies should
anyone exercise a comment the empty pages
should have told me it was time to read the tyres and
they weren't too stingy as they arrived out of nowhere
with boxes of pizzas red as sacrifice and you could close
them like a book or scatter sliced chapters on the ground for
science the way you leave your eyes

what's the damage

someone should write a history
of shoulders how much they contribute
to the economy i was thinking this last night
at westfields bondi junction the way the meat
looked so human on display those shoulders of lamb
on special not that i wanted to buy any i don't like
ovens here's a chapter – 'the shoulder in australian sport'
with subheadings that'll attract any patriot worth their
steroids; how much we loved our coppertoned shoulders
in the pre-melanoma days; up the steps in gymworld
you build the shoulder and you build a country, time to go
on a cruise and show the ocean what your mateship is made
of: in the photo your eight pairs of shoulders looked like
a rescue boat

pencil it in

borrow the grin of a prime minister
and you might be stuck with it forever
or long enough to know you've made a
mistake with your calculations of the wind's
direction; neo-phrenology's a way to go plenty
of bonework for the footloose soothsayer rafting
down olympic pool river on a someday pass;
mettle detectives saunter along burb driveways
thrusting remains of franchise cards and lead pencil
stumps towards frail tears of the raingods,
rebelieving clavicular yarns

streak

a plane flies through three chimneys easy as a view
as a child's picture book with no damage done how far
can you stretch the empirical dream; how many layers
can a logic sandwich support, the chalk always squeaked
during lectures in philosophy I; i'm not going to consider
trains exiting from fireplaces today now that time is being
served on the carved table   clothes are returning from
the laundromat covered in fresh stains this is reality not irony
– or oxymoronia, the stain economy is a growth industry
even in this age of stainless steel, books on unwelcome stains
have become best sellers, would you rather have a new bible
a folio copy of macbeth or five hundred handy tips on stain
removal it's a difficult decision; the essay asked how can
X be black and white all over, the slick answer is too grey
how many streaks can a river swim before it's a beach

knochentrocken

the guitar played on
in the food court like
a tooth recently distracted
the blockbuster movie demolished
the adjoining church before the
congregation had time to read or forgive
the credits another normal saturday at the used
car yard where the chimera keened for the quietude
of the resurrected desert, the libretto highway riddled
with the bacteria of entertainment, everyone licking at
icecream like fury in pyjamas, the random jury eulogising
the attractiveness of syrup colour at the launch of the
charitable donation pancake, the digital dog sniffing through
its plasma for the sound of a deliciously smelly bone

hill song

it was downhill all the way
until the walk back up, you
never gave much thought to
what was wrapped tight inside
the butcher's paper but you spat
the brains out on more than one occasion;
you would have lost more than half
a mark in the grammar test if you'd said
'who' instead of 'what': sawdust and chalk,
blood or feather duster, a wealth of common nouns

& the shade of anzac day from the top of the slippery
dip the ferry ploughing across the turquoise harbour
the tightening of the gut at sunset would the long day
of schooners steam the carpet with a bitter froth

the fashionable cane shopping basket an unconscious
consolation the chops and steaks and snags obscure
within the slats and you learnt to stretch your legs on
the upward climb, and took it in your widening stride
distracted by the passing views of other people's houses
the condition of their gardens the growling of their picket dogs

serial

too busy shooting blanks
to listen to the war in your feet
your infantilismo wrapped
around a tree like a confused
gauginish sook every other toe
is red or rotting mango, bravery a
blister of cheap art: male order therapy
arrives in the courier's bumbag before
grandma burns the oats

pasture

the buffet bar had only
iced corned beef and
pickle sandwiches it was
a boring novel it needed a
better murder and more full
stops the ticket inspector
carried a blue rubbish bag
in his other hand, and heated
pasties and pies to conversational
levels between announcements;
the black cattle provided some attractive
gazure and the descriptions of dostoyevsky's
sex life were absorbing though not a little
aquatic and archetypal but the moment
when he stood on a chair to get a better view
of the madonna was memorable it's always best
to travel with several books and a packet of ears
but the aeneid was too much of a big travel story
an embarrassment for this little trip to a nation's capital
the story of a woman's quest for preloved designer clothes
was on offer across the aisle for all lethargic passengers take
them home wash them and they're yours; then i had a thought
wouldn't it would be great if you could photocopy articles of
clothing you've left at the drycleaners in case they're needed
for private reasons a head's a great place to live in for a while

bookmark

the ghost swam through
the loyal grass in a voile meander
the extravagance of its weeping
shivered through the gums in search
of a more sylvan setting this
ambiguous nostalgia was really
disconcerting the anthology
reeked of too many early mornings
the cellophane flowers already sweating

blink

in the prescient vestibule
forgotten pop lyrics unfurl
in fragments, snack food
for a neglected heart, random
& compelling, unlike hotel
chocolate on a plumped up
five star pillow, smoke detectors
blink; ghost jukebox, its unexpected
visitations more affectionate than a tower
of pre-loved diaries, toppled sideways in a trunk

only the sky

a day of driving through
the longlife vermicelli is there
a better word than white the basil
perfume of your bowl the drift of prawn
in the alchemist's nook our simmering fingers
their private harps in the sudden
breezes only the sky was besmirched
by the casualness of chemicals

fleece

the chairs left the storage
colony after seven years
in the shadows with only
an opera of beggar insects for
company, they had known
death, the fine white powder
of mercantilism, they had
sniffed the greasy cargo of
an obsolete and sulking fleece;
when they left in a gold sedan
like an official pardon
they would regain their stamina
in the antique garden suburbs
of the future alert as young bamboo
with all the clairvoyance of wind chimes on
a reclining afternoon

leak

where could a trail of tissues
lead, the handkerchief was such an indiscreet
affair and burdened by its history
pinned to a breast or pocket –
users drop tissues like
old skin or five cent pieces
though ideology may prevent
sniffing in some places a possé
of nostrils may pay off for the prairie
magus if the cacti don't leak and
the horses don't crave a gymkhana

namesake

sooner or later
the dolls run out of
charisma they stare out
of their gooey cheeks bored
as mass production stills
from old news reels, celluloid
cellulite hold me in your arms
tonight, the song twangs through
the fly-drone air, their ludicrous names
some fairground mush, they'll sharpen up
as roadkill

broke

nothing out there
but a predatory sun
you can't rely on the sky
to help you sort it out it just hangs
there like a lout sucking on a milk
shake and letting it happen the burning years
are lasting longer than you would have thought when the
hoola hoop broke the sun's blister on your nose

sun scrawls like insects like a plague
we fester in our sarongs of weathered plastic
futile to read any of those scattered nappies their lethargica
too forensic & the sky no philosopher

dish

why be grateful when
you should be rude; it's
a matter of principle to
make the telephone into
a vehicle of honour speak
up for all the words that
gave you something better
than a bmw or a mc tudor
frontage, language is no
privilege for these incumbents
it's just there because it's there
like a pleasant view uninterrupted,
like a small and minor frisson to
accompany the tapestry, or a dish
of chutney to sex up any old
cold roast

rules

you stole the thunder
but you didn't qualify for
the myth, heroes don't
drink milk the way your
gob demands it; the problem
with your pronoun qualifications
is that they're under investigation,
and unlikely to qualify for any
alpine ambitions you may have googled;
history has emerged as larger and more
sophisticated than your nocturnal larceny
& scrapbook

memory loss

too many wasps in a poem
can do it ~~damage~~ justice

rum

i clipped on my custom made horse
and trotted up the south head road
like a casual centaur in search of a
moment, the lighthouse looked
too much like a brochure there on the cliff
with its white picket fence, and then the old house,
front to the ocean, back to the harbour, its
rumsmuggler history flaring the nostrils, a ninety year
old woman in the sandstone basement, damp and ancestral,
with her cockatoo general on too long a chain, watch
out for your toes; i clip-clop up to the rooms
of her nephew who believed in good fortune in a walnut
shell, i went to his 'first night of television in australia' party he
wrote a book on the subject, brian henderson glowed and
the harbour outside dark as a zoo; you could hear the corps
marching towards the shipwreck, my equine attachment
scratching the floorboards in time for a swim

novel

the emptied china cabinet waits for the painter
to move it away from the wall and then drop
the cloth over it; it's time to play the
ancestor game; a shroud in the dining room
tomorrow will remind you that you have a past,
and all the querulous behaviour inside that
cabinet so full of affection now; you turn and turn
and turn the rigid key until it locks, how beautifully
the glass shines in its vacancy, once again
so new: how occasional such relief, you could
lie down on the floor like sleep

moss

on the verge of
discovering an
interchangeability
between cause & effect
a breeze lifts the thought
like the anachronistic dandelion
of childhood information & have you
noticed how much contemporary soap
has come to resemble confectionery
& is there a dental clinic called the tooth
fairy; tootle's wheels always seemed
like lozenges of irish moss what is the relationship
between lungs and locomotives a question for poets engineers
or the medical fraternity, this word 'fraternity'
think of a fence of weathered lattice that's about to snap
leaving the timeless vine on the ground – i am the vine and
you are
the branches – didn't his words make such a pretty picture
how a poem needs stilts